Mexico

The tree-lined Paseo de la Reforma leads from Chapultepec Park into the center of the city. Among its many monuments are one to the last of the Aztec rulers, Cuauhtémoc, one to Christopher Columbus, and one to Mexican independence.

THIS BEAUTIFUL WORLD VOL. 20

Mexico

by BANRI NAMIKAWA

Published by
KODANSHA INTERNATIONAL LTD.
Tokyo, Japan & Palo Alto, Calif., U.S.A.

6-96   #134555

Distributed in Continental Europe by Boxerbooks, Inc., Zurich; in Canada by Fitzhenry & Whiteside Limited, Ontario; and in the Far East by Japan Publications Trading Co., P.O. Box 5030 Tokyo International, Tokyo. Published by Kodansha International Ltd., 2–12–21 Otowa, Bunkyo-ku, Tokyo 112, Japan and Kodansha International/ USA, Ltd., 599 College Avenue, Palo Alto, California 94306.

LCC 76–128692
ISBN 0–87011–140–x
JBC 0326–782773–2361

First edition, 1971
Second printing, 1972

Contents

Oldest Capital
in the Americas

As OUR PLANE winged its way toward Mexico City, I had the uncomfortable sensation of being lost in darkness: the only lights in the world appeared to be those inside the aircraft, while all around us loomed the inhospitable blackness of space. This sensation persisted and grew, hour after hour, as we flew through the night above the unlighted earth.

We Japanese are accustomed to our small, neat, overpopulated islands, and though we like to go off on voyages of exploration into unknown and still relatively empty parts of the world, we always, I think, do so with a certain feeling of alienation, almost of desperation; this, perhaps, was part of what I felt as the plane roared onward through the Mexican night. Then suddenly below us blazed the lights of the capital: we had arrived; we would soon be back on earth. My uneasiness vanished altogether as we went through the familiar formalities of the airport, but not my sense of strangeness, and that was never very distant during my entire stay in Mexico, a stay that lasted, as chance would have it, a great deal longer than I had anticipated. It may well be that a sense of strangeness is a useful feeling for a man to have as he looks through the eye of a camera at an unknown country.

MEXICO 🔳

Mexico is, of course, as Lesley Byrd Simpson has so ably pointed out, not one country but many countries, and here again, being Japanese, I think perhaps I was more alert to its diversity than visitors from other places where both unity and uniformity are not so highly prized as they are in Japan.

One aspect of Mexico's diversity is geographical, one historical, and both aspects are, of course, intricately interwoven to form the pattern that greets the stranger. With long coastlines on both the Atlantic and the Pacific, stretching from the temperate zone of the north across the Tropic of Cancer to the tropical jungles of the south, broken by a transverse mountainous seam that has reared active and dormant volcanic peaks rising to heights of seventeen and eighteen thousand feet, Mexico could hardly fail to be a country of physical extremes; the capital itself, lying more than a mile above sea level in the Central Plateau, is one of the loftiest cities in the world. Some regions of the country have both the heat and the tremendously heavy rainfall in which tropical forests luxuriate; others are simply barren deserts. On the coast lie rolling, grassy plains; the interior is cleft by deep valleys devoid of vegetation. Most of man's fruits and vegetables, whatever the particular climate in which they thrive, will grow in one part or another of Mexico. A ride of a few miles suffices to take one from a lush orchard or forest to an arid desert, from a fertile plain into steep mountains, from a temperate landscape to a subtropical one. Much of the country is under constant threat of devastation by earthquake and volcano.

Inevitably, this tremendous diversity has affected the history of the country. Standing at Teotihuacán one afternoon, in the merciless sunlight, I tried to transfer to some gentler, more equable climate my picture of a priest offering a still warm human heart to the sun god—and I failed. Nor must the other side of the coin ever be forgotten, for the ancient inhabitants of Mesoamerica, to quote Parkes's *History of Mexico*, "acquired a splendor which could scarcely be duplicated in Europe." Although they apparently failed to discover wheeled transport, they learned at an early stage to domesticate wild maize and then, as almost always happens after people find out how to live in one place, they progressed quickly along the road to greater and greater refinements. They built great buildings, they studied the heavens, they evolved accurate calendars, they even made use of the concept of zero before it was widely known in the Eastern Hemisphere.

The ancient ancestors of the Aztecs, the Mayas, and the Toltecs (the three most highly advanced of the pre-Columbian peoples of Mexico) crossed over to North America from Asia, presumably by way of the Bering Strait, in the dim, dark human past, perhaps ten to fifteen thousand years ago. They began moving down the continent; some got no further than the snowy north, some settled in what is now Canada, some in what is now the United States. None of these peoples ever evolved anything approaching the high civilization of those who continued further south. Many theories have been advanced as to why this should be so, but they must remain, of course, nothing but theories. Was it because those who continued on into the deserts and inhospitable mountain fastnesses of Mexico were hardier, more inquisitive people to start with? Was it because, having once learned how to cultivate maize, they stopped spending their time hunting and devoted it to more varied pursuits? What role did the diverse climate of Mexico play in these momentous developments? These are questions that have caught the attention of scholars and that still have no definite answer.

MEXICO ▓▓

To me, an Asian, one of the most irresistible facts about Mexico is that which is so ably developed by Parkes in the history that I have already mentioned. He points out how human civilization, originating in Asia, began its slow, tentative advances across the great landmasses to east and west. (Many scholars now believe that the first recognizable human being first emerged on the African continent, but I think, whether or not this is true, that it is in Asia that civilization itself must be thought of as having originated.) One migratory current moved toward the west until at last it had peopled what we now call the continent of Europe, and there, on the western fringes of the continent, it stopped. For many millennia, the Atlantic Ocean was an insuperable barrier to any further movement westward. The Asiatic peoples who roamed toward the east, however, were not stopped by an even greater ocean, for they found their way toward the north and from there, by way of the Aleutians perhaps and the Bering Strait, across to another continent, which, as the centuries and the millennia passed, they made their own. It was not until the early sixteenth century—less than five hundred years ago—in a place called Mexico that descendants of the Asiatic peoples who moved eastward met descendants of those who had moved to the west—though so far, as the visitor to Mexico soon perceives, that momentous meeting has partaken more of the nature of a collision.

Hernán Cortés, commander of the first conquistadors, called the country New Spain because of its resemblance—in climate, size, and fertility, he wrote—to Old Spain. And Nueva España it remained, until the revolutionary years of the early nineteenth century when the country won its independence. "Mexictli" appears to have been a Nahuatl word for the god of war, and the

Mexicas, or Aztecs, were members of the Nahuatl group. The capital of the Aztec Empire was México-Tenochtitlán. The Toltecs, whose capital was Teotihuacán (near Mexico City), were also members of the Nahua family; it was they, it seems, who largely developed the cult of Quetzalcóatl, a cult that the Aztecs took over as they took over so much else when they came charging into the Valley of Mexico early in the fourteenth century. They were soon its masters, but their acquired reverence for Quetzalcóatl was to contribute, before very long, to their subjugation.

On the site of the present-day Zócalo, the main square of Mexico City, the newly arrived Aztecs saw an eagle feasting on a snake, a sight they took to be so propitious that they founded their capital city, Tenochtitlán, there. The foundation was not unlike that of Venice, for the houses of the new city were built partly on islands and partly on wooden piles driven into the water. Like the Venetians, the Aztecs made good use of canals; and, again like the Venetians, they were empire builders and were soon masters of much of Mexico. Although it is, of course, unwise to stretch the analogy, one further resemblance may be noted: both peoples were sensualists, so keenly aware of the pleasures of life and so eager to enjoy them that both governments found themselves obliged to pass sumptuary laws. Is there perhaps an unexplored affinity between life on the water and the life of the senses?

One quality the two states did not share was the Aztec belief that their gods demanded vast numbers of human sacrifices. The Aztecs were almost constantly at war, since they needed a constant supply of prisoners for purposes of appeasement of the gods. As a result, the other peoples of Mexico, from whom the Aztecs drew their supply of prisoners and slaves, were disposed not only to welcome but to assist the white-skinned, bearded stranger from the sea, the incarnation, according to legend, of Quetzalcóatl, when he entered Mexico with the avowed purpose of conquering it for God and the king of Spain.

"Throughout the length and breadth of Mexico," writes Lesley Byrd Simpson, "one looks in vain for a town, village, hamlet or even a street, named after her great conqueror." The explanation for this strange lack is the fashion that has grown up "among the liberal elements to decry all things Spanish" and to encourage "a reversion to something like the good old days before the Conquest, although no one has yet had the hardihood to suggest the resumption of human sacrifice." The fact is, "Cortés was able to carry out his really awe-inspiring feat only because the bulk of the Mexican people welcomed him as a deliverer from the unbearable oppression of the Aztecs. Indeed, when Mexico City fell, it took all his address to prevent his Indian allies from slitting the throats of his prisoners. In any case it is true that Cortés put an end to Aztec power. And yet, while destroying that civilization (or, rather, its political and religious structure) Cortés became the founder of modern Mexico, unless we are willing to deny all meaning to the word. For Cortés was a builder, however much we may deplore the violence that preceded the building."*

But violence, as I was to discover for myself, is the Mexican's fairly constant companion, nor does the visitor always escape being touched by it. Perhaps this is not so very surprising, for it is a climate that seems to sow violence, and violence it has, throughout

*Many Mexicos (Berkeley and Los Angeles: University of California Press, 1966), pp. 20–23.

its recorded history, richly harvested. Stand in the Zócalo for a moment and remember all the fierce events the square has seen, from the bloodthirsty Aztecs to the sometimes equally bloodthirsty conquistadors, to almost the present day. In the Zócalo the Holy Office of the Inquisition delivered heretics to the secular arm to be burned, in the hope of saving their souls, and in the Zócalo also the Spanish established their first bullring. Here have been reflected all the fiery events that have attended Mexico's violent and largely unhappy history from its founding through the years of colonial oppression, the revolutions, the struggles for independence, the monarchies and republics, the assassinations and executions.

There is, to be sure, much more to think about, as one stands in the Zócalo, than the violence it has seen. For one thing, there is the inspiring facade of the largest cathedral in the two Americas; there is the National Palace, which was built by Cortés on the site of an Aztec palace; there is the great Aztec calendar stone, which was found very near and which, for the visitor to Mexico, is a kind of loophole onto the past. He cranes his neck to peer through, to catch a glimpse of that tortured, vanished world smoldering in the burning sun.

The calendar stone is now proudly displayed in the National Museum of Anthropology, a handsome new building in Chapultepec Park that houses many of the most important archaeological finds from more than eleven thousand locations throughout Mexico. Of these the most important of all is considered to be the calendar stone, a sculptured disk of basaltic porphyry, three feet thick, measuring twelve feet in diameter and weighing some twenty-two tons. It is not only a remarkably skillful piece of sculpture but also a remarkably accurate astronomical chart, showing powers of observation on the part of Aztec astronomers unequalled by those of ancient Greece or Rome. In the center of the stone is sculptured the sun god, while around him are the five ages of the universe. Bordering the whole stone, and facing each other at its base, are two fire serpents, for snakes, according to legend, support the sun. Within the border are other symbolic representations, including twenty hieroglyphs for the twenty days of the Aztec month.

Legend had it that Aztec life on earth was inextricably mingled with the powerful sun of the central Mexican plateau, and that the day the sun vanished from the sky all Aztec life would cease. Much of their religion, therefore, was aimed at ensuring the continued existence of the sun by taking measures to counter the exhaustion that his rigorous daily labors must necessarily induce. One of these measures—in fact, the chief one—was to offer him living human hearts.

He was not the only Aztec god who favored human sacrifice, and it was for that reason so many prisoners of war were essential to the well-being of the state. When a shortage occurred, children, young boys and girls, young men and women took their place. There were many variations on the sacrificial act: prisoners of war were usually tortured first (and eaten afterwards); children were expected to cry (and crying was considered a good omen); the young man who played the role of the god for a year was skinned after his sacrifice (and his skin was worn by a dancing priest). But in all cases, the climactic moment occurred when the victim's breast was torn open by an obsidian knife and the priest's hand reached into the cavity to pluck the hot heart forth and offer it to the deity. The archaeological museum has a stone trough in which the hearts were thrown, with suitable drainage for the blood.

It is not surprising, perhaps, that these customs made little appeal to sixteenth-century Catholic Spaniards, who had certainly seen their share, and probably more than their share, of man's seemingly infinite capacity for cruelty.

Leaving the museum we find ourselves in Chapultepec Park, one of the pleasantest spots in the capital, and one that also has witnessed critical moments in Mexican history. To the Aztecs, Chapultepec meant "Grasshopper Hill," and they had a temple at its top, at the same time making good use of the springs that gushed out at its base to supply water for the city. During the period when Mexico was New Spain, a fortress was built there, fulfilling Cortés's original intention, but the fortress was destroyed in 1847 by American troops. The memory survives in the opening words of the "Marines' Hymn."

Then, with the military backing of Napoleon III, who fancied he had inherited the talents of his famous grandfather, and with the blessing of the pope, there came the familiar tragicomic opera of Maximilian and Carlotta. Pulling the strings that animated these two imperial puppets, firm believers in the divine right of kings, were two far more potent forces: power politics and economic advantage. The United States was being racked by the tortures of civil war: it was a good moment for Napoleon, ambitious and hungry for territory, to attempt to fill the vacuum left in the New World by the departure of Spain, and a good moment also for the great colonialist landowners to destroy, once and for all, the Mexican republic. The vessels that they chose for this anachronistic task were weak ones: Archduke Maximilian of Austria was a silly young man and his wife a selfish young woman, avid for power. Their antagonist in this absurd endeavor was one of Mexico's

greatest men, Benito Juárez. The tragic end of their adventure
should have been foreseeable from the moment it began, on May 28,
1864, when under the shadow of French ordnance they landed at
Veracruz. Just over three years later, three years of sad inevitability,
Emperor Maximilian was shot, but not before he and his empress
installed themselves in Chapultepec Castle and built a fine, wide
paseo (now called la Reforma) to lead from the castle to the center
of the city. The empress, unable to secure the further intervention
of either Napoleon or the pope, went mad, as almost every movie-
goer knows, and lived on until 1927. Chapultepec Castle is now
a museum and is open to the public six days a week.

I found the capital to be a city of the most extraordinary contrasts—not only the contrast between the old city and the new (for
that, after all, is a fairly familiar phenomenon in any ancient city)
but also the contrasts among the people themselves. In the newer
and more prosperous parts of town, one sees men and women
dressed as elegantly as they would be in any other great world capital,
on their way to some luxury shop, perhaps, or to some fashionable
restaurant for lunch. Then, when one gets away from those rich
and glamorous avenues and penetrates the more popular quarters,
one sees women with *rebozos* wrapped around their shoulders and
men wearing *huaraches* (which word, I would like to think, is derived
from our Japanese *waraji*, meaning straw sandals of the kind that,
presumably, were worn by the first Japanese immigrants to Mexico).
The people you see walking the narrow streets of the poor quarters
may be inhabitants of the city, or they may be country people who
have come for their first, perhaps their only, visit to the glamorous
capital of the nation.

What a great, almost overwhelming difference there is between the two worlds! It is a gap that the government of Mexico will have increasingly to bridge if the country is to progress. The rate of unemployment is high, and that is due, certainly in part, to population growth, which also is alarmingly high. One reason for this, it seems to me, is the government's ban on artificial methods of birth control. Thus, the population of Mexico, like that of most Latin American countries, is growing far faster than the economy of the country.

As I noted earlier, violence seems to be as easy to find in Mexico as maize itself, and much violence has, to be sure, no direct economic cause (although it may well have an indirect one). It is not surprising to find some of Mexico's more pessimistic observers worried about their country's future.

Much, to be sure, has been and is being done by the government to alleviate the situation. One has only to glance at the vast housing complexes that have mushroomed all over the city to realize that the poor have not been altogether forgotten. Further, great care is being taken by the government to improve educational facilities, and school has now been made compulsory for children up to the age of fifteen; even so, the total literacy rate is only thirty-seven percent. Mexico now possesses a total of nineteen universities, some of them famous all over the world, due in part to their having been decorated by the country's world-famous artists. Mexico's modern architecture is considered to be the equal of any in the world. With all that, there are places in the capital as well as in smaller cities, towns, and villages, where the clock seems to have stopped one hundred or more years ago. Recent reforms have left the places untouched. A few miles away there may be some great *estancia*, owned perhaps by a rich politico, with a fine farmhouse, a large stable and cattle yard, a prosperous orchard; or there may be a luxury hotel with a heated swimming pool; while in the nearby village people still do not have enough to eat. Or a school to go to. Or a doctor to tend them.

To some extent, this situation must, of course, be attributed to Mexico's history, with its long, often corrupt, sometimes disastrous colonial administration, an administration that was followed by years of insurrection and revolution. Men who gained power by promises of social reform soon proclaimed themselves dictators, or even emperors. And part of the blame must be attributed to tardiness in finding a solution to the agricultural dilemma: maize, the staple that feeds the country, is also one of the most destructive of crops. Soil that has grown maize is quickly impoverished and then is good for little or nothing for several years—obviously a wasteful method of using natural resources. And part of the blame for the not entirely happy Mexican picture must be attributed to pressure from foreign capital, which has not always been interested in the well-being of the country from which it has drawn its sometimes enormous profits. And finally, part of the blame must go to the Mexican attitude toward life in general, to that state of mind that makes it easy to pull a sombrero down over one's forehead and close one's eyes against the fierce Mexican sunlight. But could any government legislate *mañana* out of the language?

For me, one of the most rewarding places to observe the daily life of the people was that peculiarly Mexican institution, the *mercado*, the market. Here daily come working-class housewives, carrying a basket into which they will eventually put the sheep's head that they will buy if the bargaining has been satisfactory. Here too come wives of men who earn higher salaries; they come in cars, which they may heap high with a week's supply of food, for these women have refrigerators and freezers at home. Nor do the markets lack their share of Mexican men either—but most of these seem to do little but engage in that ancient, time-honored occupation called girl-watching.

My first experience with a Mexican market occurred one day when I went into a cheap little eating place in a popular neighborhood and asked the owner, a plump, swarthy man, to give me something good to eat. He nodded and disappeared into the kitchen. After a little while, a woman, also plump and round faced, whom I took to be the owner's wife, appeared with a plate in her hand.

In the plate, which she set down in front of me, lay some savory-looking meatballs.

"Delicious," I said. "What is it? Chicken?"

She laughed. "Iguana," she replied. "And hard to get these days."

I recalled my first sight of these beasts in the Mexico City zoo a few days before: beady eyed and strong jawed, they may attain a length of five scaly feet and they do not look at all like the sort of beast that a human being should be eating. But then neither does the lobster, does it? I have often eaten the flesh of reptiles and have always found it excellent, as I did that day in the grimy little Mexico City restaurant. So I repeated my remark that the meat was delicious, and when I had finished, I asked the woman if there was an especially interesting market in the neighborhood.

"There's Tepito," she said. "It's a dangerous place for foreigners, but maybe since you're Japanese you'd be safe."

Somewhat reluctantly she gave me directions, which I tried to follow, but after a time I realized I was lost, so I stopped the car and asked a passing pedestrian where Tepito Market was located.

"You don't want to go there," he said flatly.

"Why not?"

"It's a den of thieves."

"I'll be careful," I assured him.

"Dangerous, too." He looked into the back of the car and saw all the cameras and other equipment. "The other day," he remarked, "a foreign photographer was murdered there."

"Really?" I said. "I didn't read about it in the newspapers."

"It's the sort of thing that happens so often at Tepito they probably didn't think it was worth printing."

Was I to believe him? It all seemed rather unlikely.

"If you go to Tepito," he added, "you'll come away with the wrong impression of Mexico."

With this I was determined to see the place. Accordingly I assured him that I would make full allowances, whereupon with a sigh he told me that Tepito was quite near and gave me exact directions for finding it. Indeed, I soon had evidence that I was approaching: the stench of decaying food was so strong I could hardly breathe. Food must, of course, be kept well refrigerated or it soon goes bad in the Mexican heat. It seemed to me that I recalled reading somewhere that Aztec nobles used to send slaves up into the mountains to bring snow back for the kitchens and the tables of the great houses.

But there was no snow at Tepito, and I wondered if there was any ice, for the odor seemed to get stronger. Buyers and sellers were still at their eternal game of bargaining; here and there on the ground, wherever there was a patch of shade, lay someone sleeping; others were eating. One man was alternately munching on some broiled meat and strumming his guitar. A woman sat with a market basket beside her, a look of utter exhaustion on her face. Everyone I saw seemed so shabbily dressed I wondered how they kept their threadbare rags together. Their expressions were unfriendly, their eyes sullen. Where, I wondered sadly, were the brave indomitable faces that the famous artists of Mexico had painted in their huge revolutionary murals? Wherever they were, they were not here at Tepito, which looked exactly like similar places I had seen in the slums of Naples and Marseilles, in the Arab countries of North Africa and the Near East, in the countries of Southeast Asia.

Displayed on the ground, in the forlorn hope of attracting buyers, lay such unlikely junk as crooked nails, shoes so worn they had lost their soles, broken neon tubes, used electric light bulbs, old and slashed tires. I decided to photograph one of these collections of rubbish, with its unprepossessing owner standing beside it, but as I was adjusting my camera I found myself surrounded, almost at once, by a large and obviously hostile mob. I admit, quite frankly, that I was frightened. I wondered whether I was going to escape with my camera or my life, and had just about decided to give my camera up but fight for my life when to my intense relief I saw the welcome figure of a policeman pushing his way through the crowd.

He escorted me back to my car. There, as I was thanking him once again for his heroic kindness, he interrupted to ask for my identity papers. I took out my wallet and was about to hand him my passport when he grabbed the wallet itself, nonchalantly abstracted all the money that was in it, and then handed it back to me.

I was so astonished I could think of nothing to say, but the policeman was not at a loss for words. "Good luck," he said, adding,

MEXICO 🔣

"I saved your life, but it wasn't worth very much, was it?" With that, he raised a rather limp hand to the visor of his cap, making a sketchy salute, and then walked off—perhaps to rescue some other lucky foreigner.

Mexican policemen, I was told, have a reputation for taking, or rather insisting on, bribes. I had an illustration of this one day when, approaching a busy intersection, I saw a traffic officer beckoning to me. I had been driving in an outer lane because I wanted to make a left turn but now had to move over to the right in order to stop near the policeman.

He asked for my driver's license, which I gave him.

Then, "You're not allowed to make a left turn at this corner," he barked.

I pointed out that there was no sign prohibiting left turns.

"No matter. I say it's prohibited, and that's that!"

"But you signaled for me to come over here."

"You could have left your car where it was and walked over."

By now I was getting angry. "Then you'd have given me a ticket for obstructing traffic."

He smiled. "And for violating parking laws."

I realized, sadly, that the stories I had been told had at least an element of truth and that I had no choice but to give him some money. Accepting ten pesos, he asked me where I was from. "Japan?" he repeated. "Well! Welcome to Mexico! I hope you enjoy your stay." He so obviously meant his good wishes that by the time I regained my car and made my left turn my anger had evaporated.

One of the few places in the world where miracles still occur is the shrine of Our Lady of Guadalupe, a few miles outside Mexico City. The story is, of course, a familiar one, but I find it so touching and so expressive of the Indian character that I would like to retell it very briefly.

It happened in December, 1531, when Our Lady of Guadalupe appeared to a poor Indian named Juan Diego and bade him tell the bishop to build her a shrine on the hill. But Juan Diego was afraid to go to the bishop with such a tale. Yet the vision appeared to Juan Diego again, and still again, and the third time, when Juan Diego expressed his reasonable Indian doubt that the Spanish bishop would believe him, Our Lady of Guadalupe said, "Give him this rose." And miraculously, though the month was December, a rose appeared.

Miraculously also, the Virgin left her likeness on Juan Diego's mantle, which was made of maguey fiber, and although the Spanish Lady of Guadalupe is clearly a European, the Mexican Lady of Guadalupe is just as clearly an Indian. In no time at all, she began performing miracles, making the blind see and the lame walk. Hers is the honor of being the patron saint of the country, and her miraculous image on Juan Diego's mantle may be seen in reproductions everywhere. She occupies the center of the high altar of the church and maintains her miraculous reputation. Science, so believers say, cannot imitate the luminosity of the colors of the original mantle, nor will the pigments permit themselves to be retouched.

The shrine is the goal of year-round pilgrimages (although perhaps less now than formerly), and in December the anniversary of the first miracle is celebrated with solemn and not so solemn rejoicing. Some of the especially pious go all the way from the Zócalo in Mexico City to Guadalupe—a distance of four miles—on their knees. Masses said in the church are always well attended; the morning I was there, in fact, the church was so crowded I wondered if I was going to be crushed to death.

Outside the church are stalls that sell food and drink, and photographers stand ready to take pictures of the pilgrims against any suitably pious background. I was fascinated, also, to watch a group of men performing an Aztec war dance—and collecting contributions from the pilgrims.

One Sunday, along with thousands of other people, I went to Xochimilco. I suppose in days long past, when it was for aristocratic Aztecs, Xochimilco had considerable elegance, but now its atmosphere is pretty much attuned to popular tastes. Large by nature, Mexican families load themselves down with babies and picnic baskets and mingle with the tourists, while everyone is importuned to keep the wheels of commerce moving: photographers and mariachis vie with boatmen and flower vendors. A fat lady with a remarkably penetrating voice was selling roasted corn; nearby, to wash down the corn, were men hawking cold beer. In Aztec days you glided down the canals on rafts converted into floating gardens; nowadays you hire a flower-bedecked boat, from which, unfortunately, holidaymakers have a tendency to toss their banana skins and orange peels into the water. The noise—of mariachis, radios, people, and babies—was overpowering; life in Aztec times must have been quieter even if slightly more ensanguined.

The most impressive of the ancient ruins in the vicinity of the capital are not Aztec at all. In fact, there is no general agreement among archaeologists as to what people actually did build the pyramids at Teotihuacán. The oldest and grandest, the Pyramid of the Sun, is thought to have been constructed by a people who lived on the plateau even before the Toltecs, the predecessors of the Aztecs, while the Toltecs are generally credited with building the lesser pyramids and the nearby temple dedicated to Quetzalcóatl.

Only thirty miles northeast of the capital, the *Zona Arqueológica* at San Juan Teotihuacán is another world altogether, formidable and frightening, unfriendly, alien, and undeniably impressive. One tries to imagine what kind of people they were who built this great pyramid and dedicated it to the blazing sun overhead, the life-giving and life-taking sun. What sort of people were they who offered it human hearts so that it would not grow weak and die— lose heart, so to speak? Did they stand in silence or did they shout as the living heart was plucked from the dead body of the victim?

Then if you climb the 248 steps to the summit, you look out over the awe-inspiring valley and then down, just below, where boys from the nearby village are having a game of *béisbol*.

Quetzalcóatl, to whom the temple was sacred, was, to quote a Mexican book on the subject, "the only god or one of the few gods that had a human precursor; that is, he was a living man before becoming a god or divinity of the Aztec religion. Aztec tradition already current twelve hundred years ago spoke of a white, bearded man, tall and powerful, wise and skillful, who preached goodness and persuaded the people to righteousness."* It was this legend, of course, that was so useful to Cortés (without his knowing it) in accomplishing the incredible feat of subduing, with a small band of men, the enormous empire of the Aztecs.

Mitos y Leyendas Mexicanas (Mexico, D.F: El Libro Español, 1963).

The temple of Quetzalcóatl at Teotihuacán is splendidly decorated with carvings of serpents' heads, for the name of the god is apparently a combination of the words *quetzal* (a bird famous for its sumptuous plumage) and *coatl* (the serpent). According to Toltec religion, which encompassed an astonishingly profound knowledge of astronomy, there occurred a highly critical time of danger for the nation every fifty-two years, and the wise and benevolent Quetzalcóatl was the god who had the power to avert the danger. When the high priest, who was also an astronomer, standing atop the pyramid, observed that the stars were continuing to behave as they were supposed to, he announced the good news that—thanks to Quetzalcóatl—the time of danger was now safely past. The Plumed Serpent, to quote the book on Mexican myths, "is the most important of the gods worshipped by the ancient Indians." He is also as much a symbol of the country as the Virgin of Guadalupe; in fact, the two deities—the bearded white god and the dark Indian virgin—are the two faces of Mexico.

1. *Glorieta de Colón* revolves around a ▶ statue of Columbus in Mexico City's Paseo de la Reforma, which claims to be modeled on the Champs Elysées.

2–3. *The capital* is an exciting analgam of old and new, of twentieth-century and pre-Columbian cultures. Above is the city's first three-level interchange; at left is a monument to the original Indian inhabitants of the country.

4. *This housing complex* in the northern part of Mexico City has fifteen thousand apartments, which will accommodate nearly a hundred thousand people, as well as schools and a hospital.

5. *"Satellite City,"* another modern development, has a remarkable monument designed by Matías Georitz to commemorate the completion of the project.

6. *Aztec Stadium*, used when the Olympic games were held in Mexico, will accomodate forty thousand spectators; surrounding shrubbery makes a highly effective setting.

7. *Work by Diego Rivera* for the Ministry of Transportation is typical both of the artist himself and of the country's twentieth-century renaissance.

8–10. *El Palacio Nacional*, standing almost in the center of the ancient Aztec capital, has huge murals by both Siqueiros (opposite) and Rivera (below).

11. *The main library* of the National Autonomous University is decorated on all four walls with mosaic murals designed by Juan O'Gorman; over seven million stones tell the story of Mexico's cultural history.

12. *This mural* in the School of Medicine, by Francisco Eppens Helguera, depicts the artist's conception of life and death and the four elements. ▶

13–16. *Chapultepec Park* surrounds the famous castle built for Maximilian and Carlota. It also has a zoo, a botanical garden, and a couple of museums.

17. *Iturbide Palace*, once the home of Mexico's first emperor (1822–23), is now given over to luxury shops.

◀18. *House of Tiles*, a sixteenth-century palace, is now the home of Sanborn's, a popular restaurant.

19–20. *Anáhuacalli Museum* was designed by Diego Rivera after pre-Columbian forms; it is a repository for native Indian art.

21. *Reflecting the course* of history, a monument from the days of the conquistadors stands like a step between ancient ruins and the tall buildings of today: foreground, ruins of pre-Hispanic pyramids; center, the sixteenth-century Church of Santiago; background, functional buildings of modern design.

41

22–25. *The Tepito* market features everything from a bent nail to a smashed automobile. Visitors are advised to leave their valuables at home.

26–27. *This city market,* like many others, has a section for native handicraft, but many of the designs are imported from abroad; the best place to buy Indian work is in the country.

28. *On Saturday*, the market at San Jacinto serves up food and music for the tourist.

29. *A woman* from the country sits patiently, awaiting a buyer for the flowers she has brought to the city.

45

30–34. *La Lagunilla* is a shopper's paradise; it also features, on Sunday mornings, a thieves' market. So here, as anywhere else in the world, let the shopper beware.

35–36. *Texcoco*, a suburb of the capital, is famous for its glassware, but many of the designs are imitations of Near Eastern originals.

37. *The Basilica of Guadalupe* was begun in 1695 on the spot where the Virgin Mary is said to have appeared to a poor Indian named Juan Diego.

38–39. *Ardent believers* approach the shrine on their knees; numerous miraculous cures have been attributed to Our Lady of Guadalupe.

40–42. *Their pilgrimage completed*, visitors enjoy watching the dances and sampling the local sweets; the image of the Virgin of Guadalupe is familiar throughout Mexico.

43–46. *Catholicism* was introduced into Mexico by the Spanish conquerors, and most of the country's churches were built during the colonial period. Mexico's colonial architecture has undoubted charms.

47–49. *Xochimilco,* fifteen miles from the capital, is where people go on Sundays to ride in flower-decked boats and then picnic —much as they might have done in the days of the Aztecs.

55

50. *The pyramids of Teotihuacán*, about an hour's drive from Mexico City, were built more than a thousand years ago by an unknown people; they were already in ruins by the time the Aztecs arrived.

51. *The walls*, both interior and exterior, were covered with brilliantly colored paintings. Jaguars were a favorite subject; the one shown here is devouring a human heart.

52. *Tula*, capital of the ancient Toltecs, fifty miles north of Mexico City,
has a series of columns cut to resemble
Toltec warriors. In the tenth century,
the Toltecs constructed a replica of
their capital at Chichén Itzá in Maya
territory, having traversed 800 miles
of jungle and plateau in their move to
the east.

Yucatán to Acapulco

I was growing impatient now to begin my long pilgrimage to the south, for the ancient ruins of southern Mexico, especially those of the Mayas, were what I wanted most to photograph. I thought I had bought and stored away in my car all the things I was likely to need, and I was ready to set out on the following morning, when I received a visit from a Mexican friend, whom I shall call Don Arturo. He had with him a small cardboard box.

"This is a parting gift for you," he said. "Keep it by your side at all times and you'll be safer than if you had a pistol or even a rifle."

"What is it?" I asked.

"A couple of hand grenades and some dynamite," Don Arturo replied.

He was not smiling, so I thanked him gravely, wondering somewhat uneasily if I was going to need his present and also how he had happened to acquire those dangerous toys. But I had found that in Mexico such questions are seldom answered and so are better left unasked.

The next morning, as planned, I left the capital, taking the new toll road that heads straight for Cholula and Puebla. After driving through a rather barren rocky region, I came upon fields of ripening maize on either side of the road. On the distant horizon, wreathed in clouds, rose the majestic peaks of Ixtaccíhuatl (17,338 feet) and Popocatépetl (17,883 feet). The ancient Indians had, of course, numerous legends associated with the White Lady and the Smoking Mountain, those two overwhelming features of the Mexican horizon, and Cortés is said to have lowered a soldier into the crater of Ixtaccíhuatl to get sulphur to replenish the Spanish supply of gunpowder during the arduous days of the conquest.

Cortés is also, of course, as most schoolboys know, intimately associated with Cholula. Though we call Cholula a village, it is actually more like a cluster of villages scattered over the countryside. When Cortés passed through, on his way to the capital, his Indian mistress, a girl named Malinche, informed him of a plot against his own life and the lives of his men. In reply, he lured some three thousand Indians into precincts sacred to the Aztecs and there massacred them. Further, atop the great pyramid of Cholula he erected a giant cross.

Long before the days of the Aztecs, Cholula had been a sacred city. Most probably it was the Toltecs who built the huge pyramid dedicated to Quetzalcóatl, the wise and gentle man-god, as well as the 400 other temples (called *teocalli*) that dotted the surrounding countryside. As an act of piety, Cortés had all 400 destroyed and—as though that were insufficient—vowed that he would build a Christian church on the site of each razed temple. He actually succeeded in fulfilling nearly half his vow: there are now about 160 churches in and around Cholula (although the local people, emulating Rome, claim that the figure is precisely 365).

Quetzalcóatl, wandering the central plateau, is said to have spent twenty years in Cholula, preaching and teaching, before he went on down to the coast and sailed away, with a promise one day to return. The pyramid erected here in his honor is the largest structure of antiquity in the New World and has dark underground passages that twist and turn but seem to have no end. The church that now stands atop the pyramid is the largest of those built in fulfillment of Cortés's vow. Baroque in style and grand in scale, it seems dwarfed by the magnitude of the pre-Columbian constructions as well as by the natural grandeur of the surrounding country.

One day, I went to visit one of the smaller churches of Cholula, one that seemed to be standing quite alone and deserted amid a field of maize. As I approached, however, I discovered that there was a fiesta going on. Under the broiling sun, a crowd of people proceeded past behind a two-man band of a trumpet and a strange, obviously handmade, stringed instrument that looked like a cross between a guitar and a ukelele. The folk in the procession sang songs in honor of the Virgin, praying for a good harvest and a happy life.

These small country churches of Cholula, by the way, constitute something of a problem for the government in its efforts to continue excavations of the pre-Columbian remains in the neighborhood. Although the churches are not of great architectural interest, they have historical and religious associations that would make the complicated process of moving them, in order to get at the structures beneath, perilously sacrilegious. Yet archaeologists believe that there are sites still to be unearthed that will rank Cholula with the ruins of Troy, the palace at Knossos, and the tomb of Tutankhamen.

I decided that I would have to leave the photographing of these revolutionary ruins for some remote *mañana*, perhaps when my grandchildren come to Mexico. I stopped only briefly in nearby

MEXICO 🪶

Puebla, which, although an extremely interesting city, is largely colonial, and I was eager to continue on to the south and the more ancient sites. One of Puebla's claims to fame is that it was here that the only partly legendary Chinese princess who was sold as a slave in Acapulco to a pious Mexican came to live, and it was in Puebla that she vowed to devote the rest of her life to good works. In order to do this, she relinquished the sybaritic silks of a Chinese princess and donned instead a rough blouse and skirt, which, now gussied up, is the national costume, the *china poblana*.

The road from Puebla to Oaxaca, a distance of some 250 miles, is good and new, though the countryside through which it passes is not of great pictorial interest. However, the end of the road, Oaxaca itself, is a fascinating place, not the least of its charms being the presence nearby of the ruins of Mitla and Monte Albán. These were the two chief reasons for my visit, but once I had experienced the attractions of the town itself, I felt inclined to settle down for an extended stay. It is an extraordinarily pleasant provincial capital, with charming outdoor life that centers around its two large plazas, where there are a number of agreeable outdoor cafés such as one finds in Spain. The town also boasts one of Mexico's most sumptuous baroque churches, made (as are many buildings in the city) of green onyx, and an archaeological museum second only to that of the capital itself. Oaxaca, incidentally, has given its name to the title conferred on Hernán Cortés as one of his rewards for conquering Mexico: he was known as the Marqués del Valle de Oaxaca. Oaxaca also saw the birth of the hero of the Mexican Republic, Benito Juárez, a descendant of Zapotec Indians.

Oaxaca is the center of two great Indian civilizations, the Zapotec and the Mixtec, and it is not always easy for the amateur

El charro comes from Jalisco.

From Nayarit, beadwork embroidery.

Mazatec style is pre-Hispanic.

China poblana is famous.

archaeologist to distinguish between the remains of the two peoples. Monte Albán, presumably the older of the two sites (and the nearer to Oaxaca), is thought to have been founded by an ancient people as their dwelling place and only later developed by the Zapotecs as a sacred city; then, not long before the Spanish conquistadors appeared on the Mexican scene, Monte Albán was presumably seized by the Mixtecs.

Monte Albán was founded on a hill, obviously for purposes of protection, but now it no longer has need of protection, and the hill affords a most glorious view of the valley. Monte Albán (White Mountain) is the name given it by the Spanish; its original Indian name was Oseotepec (Jaguar Hill-town); *tepec*, meaning "hill-town," is frequently a part of Mexican place names. There are no longer any jaguars roaming Monte Albán, but the *casahuate* trees still cover the hillsides with a blanket of white blossoms.

Monte Albán's most famous treasures were discovered in 1932 by Professor Alonso Caso in one of those dramatic breakthroughs that make the history of archaeology so tantalizing and exciting. Not quite perhaps on a level with the discoveries of Mycenae, Troy, and Knossos, Professor Caso's Tomb 7 has proven to be a trove of treasures of intense artistic as well as historical interest. Most of them are housed now in Oaxaca's museum and give unquestioned proof of Zapotecan skill in goldsmithery. The general opinion is that Tomb 7, built by the Zapotecs, was taken over by the Mixtecs as a royal mausoleum. One of the mysteries of Monte Albán is the large number of carvings of deformed people; Professor Caso explains them as evidence of miraculous cures, but so far that is only a hypothesis.

Mitla, the city of the dead, about twenty-five miles south of

Oaxaca, has given the world no goldwork or other jewelry to compare with that of Monte Albán, and archaeologists suppose the explanation to lie in looting by Spanish conquerors and settlers. However, the mausoleums of Mitla are faced with stone mosaics in geometrical patterns of an almost incredible intricacy, giving further proof that the people who lived in the Valley of Oaxaca before the appearance of its marquis were craftsmen as skilled as any that the world has ever known.

A little over 150 miles to the southwest of Oaxaca, just north of the Pacific port of Salina Cruz, lies the not very attractive but undeniably strange, in some ways unique town of Tehuantepec—unique because its women, Mexico's famous *tehuanas*, outnumber its men by a quite extraordinary ratio, perhaps five to one, and because it is the women who run the town. They are also taller and, so it would seem, stronger than the men and wear fancy, colorful costumes while the men dress drably. The women of Tehuantepec would have qualified magnificently for inclusion in John Knox's condemnation of "the monstrous regiment of women," but happily the women of Tehuantepec are quite ignorant of sixteenth-century Scottish preachers and admirably satisfied with their own position in the twentieth-century world of southern Mexico.

Continuing on, I stopped briefly at the town of Juchitán—where I met a witch. In any event, the local name for her was *bruja*, a word familiar to any admirer of Spanish music. Like the other women of Juchitán and nearby Tehuantepec, she was large, solidly built and brilliantly dressed in bright primary colors. Like her sisters, she went barefoot, but unlike them she had other things to do than tend to the mundane business of the town. The other women were busy drawing water or carrying loads, running the market and the shops

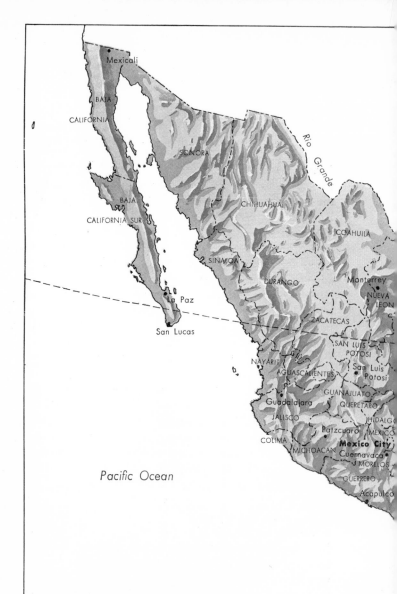

THE UNITED STATES OF MEXICO

Matamoros

Gulf of Mexico

————— Tropic of Cancer — — — — —

MAULIPAS

Tampico

Merida YUCATAN

XCALA
uebla   Veracruz   Campeche   QUINTANA
UEBLA VERACRUZ   TABASCO   ROO
                       CAMPECHE
                Villahermosa
Oaxaca
OAXACA   Juchitan
Tehuantepec   CHIAPAS
              Tonala

MEXICO

(while the men, what were left of them after local feuds had taken their toll, slept or rested from a surfeit of sleep), but the *bruja* merely sat waiting for clients. Their wants were diverse: one man might ask her to cast a spell over another man for whom his girl had taken a fancy; someone else might hire her to make a straw effigy of an enemy and pierce its heart with a needle; a woman might (for reasons of her own) require "medicine" that would drive her husband crazy or make him impotent. For all of these contingencies the *bruja* had her herbs, her spells, and her specially prepared concoctions—among them a liquor made of the genitalia of a snake dried and ground. I must report that, despite the heat, I declined her kind offer of a drink.

I continued on to Guatemala and Honduras because I wanted to see the Mayan ruins in the jungles at Tikal and Copan. On my way back, for reasons of expediency, I left my car behind, and as our train meandered through jungles and cactus fields, I thought how pleasant it was to leave the driving to someone else for a change. Soon we arrived at a little country station, and as it was such a flimsy affair, with only a tiny hut serving as the station house, I supposed that we would be there for but a very short time.

I supposed, however, wrong. Little boys were soon at all the windows, selling the fruits of the region—mangoes, papayas, bananas, and the like—and my fellow passengers, plump ladies and mustachioed gentlemen, were soon contentedly munching away. One young man got his guitar down from the rack and began strumming on it; others, moved by the music, carefully drew bottles out of their sacks and the train was soon redolent of the stong smell of fermented and distilled cactus.

I dozed off. I have no idea how long I slept, but when I woke the sun seemed to be on the other side of the train. Other passengers were having a siesta, but the musical young man was still strumming his guitar. "Hola, you from Japan!" he cried, when he saw that I was awake. "Let's go see what the trouble is."

We lowered ourselves to the ground and went up to the engine. But the only person to be seen was a watermelon vendor.

"Where is the engineer?" I asked.

"At the fiesta of course," answered the other.

So we too, of course, went to the fiesta, where we found the engineer drinking and singing with friends. Later in the afternoon we all returned to the train; the steps of my guitar-playing acquaintance were by then rather uncertain, and the engineer was in a jolly mood.

The passengers we had left behind in the train were not. In fact, they gave the engineer—not to put too fine a point on it—hell.

He explained that he had been at the fiesta in the village, and the other passengers found his explanation so reasonable that they promptly left the train and went to the fiesta too.

"They were angry," said the engineer, speaking somewhat too carefully, "because I didn't take them along."

"What will happen now?" I asked.

"Oh, they'll be back in the morning," he replied airily. "You see, the fiesta will go on all night."

"But what about the train? Aren't you going to start it again?"

"Of course! After all the passengers get back."

My immediate reaction, one of intense fury, soon vanished, when I saw everyone having such a good time. After all, I had no tight schedule to meet. And neither, obviously, did they.

The next morning everyone returned to the train carrying huge bunches of bananas and bottles of spirits, and everyone, including the engineer, was rather more than a bit drunk. But the train was so old and traveled so slowly that I had no great fear, even though it was quite clear that the engineer could hardly see the track. And indeed, we reached our destination safely, I retrieved my car, and continued on to photograph the ruins of the great buildings that ancestors of my jolly traveling companions had built so many centuries ago.

I do not want to give the impression that travel in Mexico, once you leave the capital, is merely like trying to use a network of antiquated and decrepit streetcars; one of the marvels of the country is the skill of its engineers in constructing wide, modern highways under sometimes appalling conditions. One such is the broad road that links Villahermosa to Campeche and passes not far from the ruins of Palenque—and passes also, incidentally, through miles and miles of jungle and swamp. It is a miracle of engineering, a tribute to Mexican skill, and a boon to the traveler eager to see some of the more inaccessible Mayan ruins.

Villahermosa, the capital of the State of Tabasco, is a pleasant town of some sixty thousand without a great deal to attract the traveler save its museum of regional antiquities. Most of them come from excavations at La Venta, about seventy-five miles to the east, almost on the Gulf of Mexico, and some of the finds made there date from two thousand years ago, or perhaps more.

On the other side of Villahermosa, on the way to Campeche, lies the village of Palenque and near it the ruins that revolutionized scholarly thinking about the Mayas. It was in 1952 that the Mexican archaeologist, Professor Alberto Ruz, investigating the pyramid upon which stood the so-called Temple of the Inscriptions, discovered a burial vault. In its center was a sarcophagus containing the bones of a dead priest and a huge treasure of jade, the most valued possession of the Mayas. This was the first time that a tomb was ever found in a Mayan pyramid: until Professor Ruz's discovery, the pyramids of the Mayas were thought to have no connection with their burial customs.

Palenque, which flourished in the seventh century, is unique in other ways. Its temples are more refined and delicate than temples found in other Mayan sites, and it is also unusual in that its hieroglyphic texts are recorded, not, as is customary, on stelae, but on the walls of the buildings themselves. Another Palenque rarity is the considerable and very beautiful use of stucco for decorative purposes as well as to communicate necessary information.

Much of the stucco has, of course, vanished with the centuries, for Palenque stands amid a jungle so humid that one immediately compares it to a sauna bath. Enclosed rooms are like grottoes of stalactites, with water dripping incessantly from the ceiling. It is a most impressive sight and makes one wonder, as do almost all the ruins of the Mayas, how these people were able to build their splendid, sumptuous cities in the midst of jungles and what impelled them then to leave the cities and build again elsewhere.

Properly speaking, of course, they were not cities at all. That, as noted in the chapter on the Mayas in *Vanished Civilizations*, "is a misnomer, for they were not urban centres, but the religious and administrative capitals of districts; the usual term is ceremonial centre. . . . Apparently, it had no permanent population, for the people lived in small settlements scattered over the surrounding country, coming to it for important religious feasts, courts of

MEXICO 🙵

justice, markets and in connection with the civic administration of
the district."*

Such then, were the manifold purposes of these centers scattered
over southern Mexico, Guatemala, and Honduras; and to accom-
plish these purposes the Mayas evolved a highly complex system of
hieroglyphics and a calendar of incredibly elaborate accuracy as well
as diverse methods of building that enabled them to make each
ceremonial center unique.

The complex calendar tables, Dr. Thompson continues, "the
great probings scores of millions of years into the past, the arith-
metical calculations which involved the invention of a symbol analo-
gous to that of zero, and the whole concept of the eternity of time
because it is cyclic were extraordinary intellectual achievements
without parallel among peoples on a similar cultural level throughout the history of the world."* Yet on the practical level the Mayas
suffered from "extraordinary failures": they failed to evolve wheeled
transport (along with all the other aboriginal peoples of North and
South America), they failed to evolve a true arch, they failed to
evolve the use of scales for weighing, most serious of all they failed
to evolve means of feeding their people adequately and keeping
them healthy. For one, or all, of these reasons, or for still other reasons, this remarkable civilization disappeared from the living history
of man, leaving behind only deserted ruins, threatened by the
ever-encroaching jungle, to which come the present-day descend-

*J. Eric S. Thompson, "The Gods That Failed: The glory and decay of
Maya culture," in *Vanished Civilizations: Forgotten Peoples of the Ancient
World,* ed. Edward Bacon (London: Thames and Hudson, 1963), pp.
159, 164.

72

ants of the Mayas, offering prayer and sacrifice to the ancient gods
without quite knowing who they were.

Between Palenque and the Mayan strongholds of Yucatán the
chief stop is Campeche, a town of about fifty thousand and the
capital of the State of Campeche. The word (so I was told) means
"ticks and snakes" in the local language, and while the town itself
is a pleasant one, Campeche is an extremely descriptive name for
much of the state. There seem to be literally scores of different
kinds of snakes with, no doubt, different degrees of virulence
(which I hoped not to experience), and there are scores of billions
of sand ticks that energetically and painfully sting the hot and weary
traveler who goes down to the beach for a cooling walk or a swim—
or to admire the transcendent glory of the sunset. Then even the
sand ticks are forgotten. Never anywhere else have I seen nature,
evening after evening after evening, offer quite so stupendous a
display. Just before sinking into the waters of the Gulf of Mexico,
the sun suddenly turns from golden red to flaming crimson and
incarnadines both sky and sea, making—to paraphrase a remote
Elizabethan playwright—the blue as well as the green one red.
Then onto the crimson sea glide native dugouts roofed with coconut
leaves; the people in the little boats wear hats made out of woven
leaves of the banana-plant.

The Classic Age of Mayan civilization flourished until the tenth
century. Then, for some reason as yet undetermined, the great ceremonial centers of the past were largely abandoned, and Chichén
Itzá was occupied by Toltecs from Tula, some fifty miles north of
Mexico City. Now the arts of peace among the Mayas declined as
the art of war gained an ascendency it had never possessed before:

the Toltecs introduced into Mayan life the worship not only of Quetzalcóatl but also of other, less gentle gods who required their ration of human hearts. The Mayas now adopted the northern custom of waging war for the purpose of taking as many prisoners as possible, since the more sacrifices that were made, the more certain it was that the sun would emerge from his nightly death and would weather the periodical crises that threatened his existence.

After two centuries of ascendency Chichén Itzá fell and was replaced by a new capital, Mayapan. This was not a mere ceremonial center but a true city, with numerous dwellings as well as temples and other public buildings. It is thought to have been a kind of military dictatorship, and, as is only to be expected, art and architecture further declined during the period of Mayapan supremacy. The rulers of the city failed in their attempts to conquer the entire peninsula. In the year 1460 the Mayas revolted, pillaged the city, and overthrew the dictatorship. Then, for a century Yucatán was divided into a number of small states, until, in the 1550s, the conquering Spanish founded a new capital, called Mérida. The last Mayan stronghold, Tayasal, fell to the Spanish in the last year of the seventeenth century.

Mérida remains a Spanish colonial city of great charm, far and away one of the most attractive cities in the whole country, but one is also aware of the fact that it is a Mayan capital. The ancient Mayas apparently developed a distinctive physical type, and present-day Yucatecs are just as eager as their ancestors were to preserve it. "We are not true Mexicans," said one friend I made there. "The blood of the Mayas is still pure and unadulterated in our veins, and we want to keep it that way."

I was interested to learn that it is a custom among the men of

54. *Acacoyagua*, in the State of
Chiapas, saw Mexico's first Japanese
immigrants, who helped clear the
jungle; their descendants are improv-
ing local rice cultivation.

55. *This "drugstore"* stocks such panaceas as calf foetus, dried starfish and baby shark, and powdered armor of an armadillo.

56. *Women*, well padded and brilliantly dressed, do most of the work in this small village on the border between Oaxaca and Chiapas; among them are witches and faith healers.

57. *Monte Albán*, near Oaxaca, former capital of the Zapotec Indians, offers some of the most beautiful and fascinating remains in all America.

58. *Inhabitants* nearby are thought to be descendants of either the Olmeca of Monte Albán or the Zapotecs of Mitla; they are noted for their weaving.

59. *Mitla, a* few ▶ miles away, became an important capital after the decline of Monte Albán.

61. *Temple of the Sun*, standing in the midst of a luxuriant jungle, is representative of the Classical Age of Mayan culture.

60. *Palenque*, on the border between the states of Chiapas and Tabasco, boasts Mayan ruins dating back a thousand to fifteen hundred years.

62. *Mayan writing* is still largely a mystery, although certain words have been deciphered—mainly names of people and places; the relief below is from Petén.

63. *Campeche*, on the western coast of the Yucatán Peninsula, offers a spectacular view of the setting sun —seen here with a sudden squall rising.

64. *Gray pelicans* migrate to the Campeche district from the Caribbean every June. ▶

65. *A young man* on his way to work in the hemp fields; in Campeche a boy becomes a man (and does a man's work) as soon as he can grow a moustache.

66. *The State of Yucatán* has few
rivers and depends for its water supply on wells; windmills pump the
water up.

67–68. *The soil of Yuca-tán* is well suited to the cultivation of sisal, the fiber of which is used for rope making, among other things.

69. *Kabah*, close-by, is the site of another very impressive Mayan ruin, this one dedicated to the god of rain; in this typical relief, he is depicted with large round eyes and a hooked nose.

70. *Uxmal*, about fifty miles south of Mérida, has some of the best preserved of all Mayan buildings.

71. *The ruins of Sayil*, a few miles south of Uxmal, are typical of one style of Mayan architecture; the material is limestone.

72. *Most extensive* of all Mayan remains are those at Chichén Itzá, eighty miles east of Mérida, first capital of the New Mayan Empire.

73. *This cenote de sacrificios* was a well sacred to the important god of rain; periodically human sacrifices were hurled into the well, along with jewelry and other articles of value.

74. *A ball-court relief* shows captain of winning team at left, vanquished (and headless) captain at right; the blood spurting from his neck is stylized in the form of snakes.

75. *El Tajín*, in the State of Veracruz, has a pyramid seven stories high with 365 niches.

76. *This relief in* the ball court is highly complex and typical of El Tajín decoration.

Yucatán to divorce a wife who does not bear children. Presumably a barren marriage is always the wife's fault—just as it used to be in Japan. A young woman told me quite frankly that she was going to divorce her husband and let him marry someone else because she had not borne him any children. "The blood of our people," she said, "is more important than personal happiness. Individuals live and die, but the Mayan race must not be allowed to perish." Although the young lady appeared to accept the dissolution of her marriage stoically, I was far from sure that I agreed with her that blood is more important than happiness. Still, it is an old-fashioned concept that was prevalent in a large part of the world once, and it suggests how much more old-fashioned Mérida tends to be than the rest of Mexico.

A city of some two hundred thousand, Mérida has, to be sure, a sufficient number of taxis, but its citizens prefer horse-drawn carriages, and the roll of the wheels and the clatter of hooves make a very pleasant change from the motorized roar of most cities. (There are also people who prefer the smell of horses to the stink of exhaust fumes.)

The first impression Mérida makes upon the visitor is one of cleanliness: in this it is different from other Mexican cities, and Yucatecs, who are proud of this quality in themselves, make every effort to foster it, despite the fact that they live in an extremely hot, humid, and enervating climate. They also, in spite of their climate and their land, have a rich, varied, and distinctive cuisine, of which they are equally proud. Their staple, of course, is maize, which they eat at virtually every meal, but they also have such delicacies as chicken barbecued in banana leaves, turkey stuffed with pork, and venison cooked in a variety of ways.

MEXICO ▦

One of the plants that thrive in the hot, moist climate of Yucatán is the agave, from which the people make a fiber named after the Yucatecan port of Sisal (the fiber is also called henequen), and out of it they weave all manner of things, from hats to shoes, from mats to hammocks. The fiber is also exported to make an extremely sturdy rope.

Emphasizing the fact that they do not care in the least whether they are considered old-fashioned or not, the citizens of Mérida are much given to rocking chairs (which help create a breath of air in the hot stillness), to windmills (which draw water up from deep underground), and to *confidentes* in their public squares. The latter are **S**-shaped, stone love seats and are carefully placed in dim corners; presumably this is a good way for young men and women to become acquainted and, in the course of time, contribute to the preservation of the Mayan race.

The Yucatecs carry their feeling of independence from the rest of Mexico to the point where they do not always recognize official documents issued by the federal government in the capital. My permit to photograph ancient Mexican remains was, I was told, not valid in Yucatán: I had to secure special permission from the state.

Mérida is, of course, the obvious center for visiting, and photographing, the Mayan remains on the peninsula. To facilitate matters, I rented a jeep, because many of the sites are not easily accessible, some of them being well off the roads in dense jungle. When we arrived, hot and panting and craving a cold drink (the water that we carried was by this time almost as hot as we were), I understood why so many buildings were sacred to the god of rain.

The best-known and best-preserved site in the region is the relatively late center of Chichén Itzá; it is also the easiest to get to and even boasts a luxury hotel, with a swimming pool. As we have already noted, the Chichén Itzá that has come down to us was largely rebuilt under Toltec influence and domination. Uxmal, the other well-known center of Yucatán, is more authentically Mayan and shows no suggestion of a Toltec presence. The long nose of Chac, the Mayan rain god, is a conspicuous feature of Uxmal's sculpture, and the geometrically patterned mosaics are remarkable. In the opinion of some scholars, Uxmal's House of the Governor is not only the handsomest but also the best-preserved building in any Mayan center.

I visited also such lesser sites, all in the Mérida region, as Kabah, Sayil, and Labna. All Mayan sites have their distinctive characteristics and all are fascinating to visit, but to attempt merely to list the various remnants of temples and pyramids would be far beyond the scope of these brief notes. One thing all the sites had in common was a sculptural passion for time and the calendar. To give some idea of what this meant in the daily life of the people, I can do no better than quote once again from that distinguished Maya scholar, Dr. Thompson:

"The core of the elaborate Maya calendar was a divinatory almanac of 260 days, formed of concurrent cycles of 20 names and the numbers 1 to 13, both names and numbers being divine beings whose day of joint rule affected all mankind according to their natures. The whole life of the community revolved around this succession of good, bad, and indifferent days; priests were kept busy deciding what combination of day name and number was most suitable for every undertaking—sowing, taking honey from hives, hunting, curing illness, marrying, or making war. . . .

"It seems a logical deduction," Dr. Thompson continues, somewhat later, "that the Maya with their probings into the past and their measuring of greater and greater reentering cycles of time had developed the idea that time had no beginning. Set against the belief current in western Europe until a century ago that the world was hardly six thousand years old, this was an astonishing intellectual advance."*

The last Mayan site I visited was El Tajín, in the state of Veracruz, near the town of Papantla. The pyramid of El Tajín, which was discovered toward the end of the eighteenth century, is well over fifty feet high and has a total of six stairways and 365 niches. There are a number of other sites in the district waiting to be excavated, but the government (sadly but naturally) prefers to spend its money and effort excavating and exploiting the oil that lies under the sites. Wherever necessary, jungles are being ruthlessly cleared by dumping tons of waste oil on them and then setting it alight; the burning oil does not attack merely the lush green vegetation of the jungle, it destroys the roots of the plants and trees. A rainstorm may put the fire out, but the oil remains, and after the rain has ended a match is enough to start the jungle blazing again. Then once the growth has been cleared away, the ground is leveled by bulldozers and made ready for the construction of oil refineries, which, in Mexico, are all operated by the government. My last view of Mexico's ancient Maya-land was black smoke belching from man-made fires against a sullen gray sky.

Back in Mexico City again, I made preparations for the next trip

*J. Eric S. Thompson, op. cit., p. 163.

—this one comparatively easy, for it was to be made, for the most part, on the broad highways that link the capital with other chief cities in the Central Plateau and with the Pacific coast. The chief obstacle, I had been told, was a number of hairpin curves on the mountain passes, where drivers all too frequently lost control and plunged to their deaths down the steep cliffs. So my wife, my assistant, and I set out lightheartedly for what we anticipated was going to be an easy and pleasant journey to Mexico's second city, Guadalajara.

Aside from the stark, imposing mountains of the Great Seam, which stretches from the Gulf of Mexico to the Pacific, the Central Plateau seems to be made up chiefly of two different kinds of soil: green and fertile land, which is given over to pasture, and dry, barren earth where little will grow but maize, the staple of the country. Owners of large *estancias*, with thousands of head of cattle, are of course well-to-do, if not outright rich, while maize farmers often subsist in the most abject poverty.

We took the northern route across the plateau, which brought us as far as San Luis Potosí, a pleasant colonial city with a number of attractive pink churches and a narrow street of shops reminiscent of Seville's Sierpes, and then we headed southeast toward Guadalajara. All went well until just before we entered the town of Tepatitlán, when we were deluged by a sudden gusty rainstorm that reduced visibility to almost zero. Naturally enough, my assistant, who was driving at the time, slowed down, but, a few moments later, in swerving to avoid a car that suddenly appeared from in back of an oncoming truck, he lost control.

When I came to, I found myself still in the car, but the car was no longer on the road; it had slid down an embankment of red dirt, and the dirt was still gently raining down on us. Although the whole right side of my body was numb, I managed to get my wife, who was still unconscious, up to the road just as a large cattle truck was approaching. I signaled it to stop, and several men got down and helped me to bring my assistant up to the road; then the truck went off to summon an ambulance for us. It arrived in about thirty minutes.

My traveling companions were put on stretchers and carried to the ambulance, while I was told to sit beside the driver. He said I could not be in such bad shape if I could still talk. Instead of a doctor, there was a priest who kept sprinkling the three of us with holy water as he muttered prayers. "Stop that!" I cried angrily. "We're not Catholics. God and prayers are all very well, but why didn't you bring a doctor?"

"I'm the one who can save you," the priest replied coolly, "not a doctor."

By that time we had arrived at the Red Cross first-aid station in Tepatitlán, where we were given blood transfusions and injections to ease our pain. In a little while a hearse arrived, and when I asked who had died, I was told the hearse was for us. The doctor sent it away, declaring we were all out of danger, but we did have to spend about four months in a hospital in Guadalajara, where we were cared for by Dr. Hiramuro, a Mexican of Japanese ancestry.

I suppose Japanese are not very different from other people: when they are in trouble, they like to have their own countrymen around. A number of other Guadalajarans of Japanese ancestry came to visit us while we were in the hospital, unable to leave our beds most of the time, and they could not have been kinder to us. At the same time, and in this way, we came to know and admire the people of Mexico—our Japanese-Mexican friends acted as a kind of bridge—and we shall never forget their kindness. We decided that, although Mexicans may not be the fastest-moving people in the world, they are certainly among the most well-meaning and considerate.

When, at last, we were able to leave the hospital and continue our voyage of exploration, we found Guadalajara to be the most agreeable of Mexican cities—not so bustling and modern as the capital but with plenty to amuse the visitor and with an atmosphere that is thoroughly individual. It is a well-to-do city, the capital of western Mexico and the financial center for the cattle and rich agricultural country. And what is more, Guadalajara looks well-to-do, with its delightful main square (the Plaza Mayor), its many smaller tree-shaded squares, its splendidly modernistic market, its outdoor cafes, and its many excellent hotels both old and new.

Another major attraction of Guadalajara is that the painter Orozco lived there and left much of his finest work there, in the Palacio del Gobierno, in the Hospicio Cabañas, and in his own house, which is now a museum.

Then there is the fascination of Tlaquepaque, in the suburbs of the city (about two and one half miles from the center), which combines pottery making (largely for the tourist) with outdoor night life (largely for the Mexican). The pottery, in fact, I found rather coarse and the prices outrageously high, but the mariachis were an endless delight. Tlaquepaque has a vast number of open-air cafés, to which the people of Guadalajara (and much of Mexico as well) come to drink and drown in the saccharine ballads of the mariachis. Sometimes there are so many bands playing simultane-

ously that it is quite impossible to distinguish one tune from another.
But it is fun all the same; Mexico enjoys it, and so did we.

More interesting than Tlaquepaque, from the point of view of
Mexican handicraft, is Tonalá, a little further out. The products
themselves may be no more refined, but the place is less touristy,
and it is pleasantly interesting to go from one atelier to another,
watching the various processes involved in the making of pottery
and glassware.

We even went all the way up to the town of Tequila, some forty
miles northwest of Guadalajara, to pay our respects to the birth-
place of Mexico's national drink. It is not, I hasten to add, that
any of us was overwhelmingly addicted to this peculiarly Mexican
beverage, although we found it pleasant enough when drunk, as
Mexicans often do, with lemon and salt. I think we were mainly
curious to see what a town named Tequila would look like.

Actually, as I learned, the drink was discovered quite by ac-
cident in Amatitlán, an impoverished village not far from Tequila.
Here, in the eighteenth century, there was a great fire that destroyed
all the houses in the district, and much of the cattle, and, as it happened, some of the maguey fields. Other fields were only partly
burned, and the hungry people of the region, once the fire was out,
tried eating some of the partly burned plants and found the meat
very good, like extremely sweet brown sugar, but they were still a
long way from distilling it.

It was the Spanish colonialists who took that step. They experi-
mented with the stalks of this variety of maguey, extracted its
juice, and then, in the town of Tequila built a factory to distill it.
So agreeable was this new drink that they obtained permission
from the governor-general of Nueva España to market it on a

large scale. It was called, for a time, "the drink of New Spain."

Of course, the native Indians of Mexico had a fermented maguey drink long before the coming of the Spaniards. This, which they make from the juice of the agave or a different species of maguey, they called, and still call, pulque. The milky juice of the plant is tapped just before the buds begin to open and, after the process of fermentation, has an alcoholic content of around fifteen percent. Not very high perhaps but enough—as any visitor to Mexico knows —to have an effect.

The road back to the capital took us along the shore of Lake Chapala and across the State of Michoacán, the home of the Taras-can Indians. Chapala has been written about so extensively and is so familiar to all visitors to Mexico that I shall confine my remarks to saying I agree with the majority: it is an extremely peaceful and beautiful lake, and I quite understand why so many artists and writers have retired to the villages, Ajijic in particular, that dot its shore. Some of them, it seems, actually do some work, but it is easy to see how other, less determined people might be content just to paddle around the lake, drink beer, and think about doing some work *manaña*. There are worse ways to spend one's time.

The state line between Jalisco and Michoacán crosses the eastern end of the lake, and beyond the border lies Tarascan land. How these Indians got the name by which they have been known since the Spanish conquest is another example of the misunderstandings— in this case, happily, not a serious one—that result when two widely different cultures encounter one another. Apparently the story is a true one. When the conquering Spaniards first came into Michoacán, the Indians dwelling there, desirous of fraternizing with the conquerors, offered their daughters in marriage. "Tarasca, Tarasca," said the Indian fathers: "Son-in-law, son-in-law." And they said it so often the Spaniards decided it was the name of the people, and by that name they have been known ever since.

They are, I found, among the most interesting of Mexico's Indian groups—people who have maintained their individuality and their ancient customs and who live, incidentally, in some of the most attractive country in Mexico, particularly around Lake Pátzcuaro. Their ancient capital had the delightful name of Tzintzuntzan, which means place of hummingbirds; then, in the early fourteenth century, they founded the more modern city of Pátzcuaro. Excavations made recently in the center of the town revealed a Tarascan tomb with a great treasure of gold and jewelry—perhaps the tomb of the founding father.

The town itself is a pleasant place, with an enormous (and famous) mural by Juan O'Gorman, but the chief interest is, of course, the nearby lake and the Island of Janitzio. We hired a canoe to take us out there, spurning a decrepit and noisy motorboat, and enjoyed the leisurely ride across the quiet water, with Tarascan fishermen in the distance deftly handling their famous butterfly nets. What they were fishing for, I was told, was a catch known simply as *pescado blanco*, "white fish," a species well regarded throughout the Central Plateau.

After we arrived on the island, I explained that we were photographers who had come all the way from distant Japan, and at that we were given as openhearted a welcome as any photographer could possibly desire. The men immediately began preparations to perform what I understood to be an old man's dance, the purpose of which was to preserve the dancers' virility, enabling even the oldest of men to beget children. The costumes, white embroidered in red, were very handsome; the dancers wore pink masks and hats with yellow streamers. The movements of the dance seemed rather simple but perhaps that was just as well for old men who were anticipating more serious exertions later.

Whether or not one is deeply impressed by their dancing skill, one must admire the dexterity and variety of Tarascan handicraft. In this they reminded me of the artisans of my own country. Near Uruapan are villages that specialize in woodwork. Most Mexican guitars are manufactured there, and one village is known throughout the country as "the three-peso village," because the simple chairs the people make sell for around three pesos each. (That works out to around twenty-five American cents.) Another famous Tarascan craft is the making of mats out of the local reeds, which are then dyed in brilliant colors. I think no country in the world equals Mexico in the variety of its folkcrafts, and for this achievement the Tarascans may take a major share of the credit.

At Uruapan, the town's main industry is lacquer ware, and some of the work is so fine one quite forgets the unattractive origin of the lacquer itself—it is a gum made out of a plant louse and requires a great deal of working and rubbing. The end result is extremely durable, and some of it, as I say, is very handsome and of obviously Indian inspiration. Uruapan is clean and green once again, after eight years (from 1943 to 1951) of being showered night and day with volcanic ash from Paricutín. The volcano is now said to be extinct, but I doubt whether any volcanologist guarantees that it will stay that way.

Our last Mexican journey was the familiar, sometimes too familiar

Rich veins of folklore and history are tapped for modern dance themes: a prehunt dance of the Yaqui Indians (*upper left*); a story from the 1910 Revolution (*upper right*); Mayan (*lower left*) and Aztecan (*lower right*) themes.

one that includes those lovely but tourist-ridden cities of Cuernavaca, Taxco, and Acapulco. Of the pleasures of Cuernavaca, the beauties of Taxco, the fun of Acapulco I shall keep my remarks to a minimum, for they are all there; everything that one has been promised is true.

Cuernavaca is indeed one of the pleasantest places in the world, with a superb climate, far easier to live with than the more elevated climate of the capital, as so many people have discovered. My only regret was that the huge mural Siqueiros is doing for one of the luxury hotels was not yet visible, since I have always considered him one of the most exciting of painters and one of the greatest of Mexicans. His life is a fabulous mixture of art and politics, and it is sometimes impossible to guess where, in his thinking, one ends and the other begins. He was a leading figure in the political orientation of Mexican painters, he fought against Franco in the Spanish Civil War, he quarreled with Rivera after the assassination of Trotsky, a quarrel that was loud and well publicized, but he was also one of the chief mourners at Rivera's funeral; he has been jailed for his political activities, he is extremely popular, and—most paradoxically Mexican—proclaims himself a Communist, wears blue workingman's clothes, and drives a Mercedes-Benz.

Then, Taxco—what is one to say about Taxco that has not already been said? It too is one of the pleasantest places in the world, it too has a lovely climate, and it too has attracted a number of foreign residents—artists on the whole rather than, as at Cuernavaca, the well-to-do. I paid a visit to the house of Tamiji Kitagawa, the Japanese painter who lived, worked, and taught in Taxco for fifteen years. I enjoyed the nighttime fireworks that illuminate so splendidly the baroque facade of Santa Prisca, the church that was paid for by a French miner, Joseph le Borde, who found a fabulously rich vein of silver. The Mexicans changed his name to Borda and said of him, "God gives to Borda and Borda gives to God."

Just outside of Taxco I saw, for the first and only time in Mexico, rice being cultivated. To a Japanese it is one of the most familiar sights in the world and for the first time since I embarked on my endlessly fascinating tour of Mexico I felt a flash of homesickness and, for a moment, was almost glad that my tour was approaching an end.

It was just outside Taxco that I saw a group of women and children standing beside the highway, all holding bulky, apparently heavy objects aloft. I stopped the car, and we got out. The objects were iguanas and armadillos being offered for sale. The armadillo shell, I was told, was customarily dried and then powdered to be used as a cure for asthma. The iguana, as I knew, was considered a culinary treat, and I wondered again, as we watched the animals, why people were prejudiced against eating the flesh of reptiles. After all, birds and reptiles are closely related on the evolutionary scale, and the flesh of reptiles, which I have eaten often in out-of-the-way and not so out-of-the-way places, does indeed resemble that of various fowl. Turtle soup is a well-known delicacy; less well-known but equally delicious are such things as broiled alligator's tail, turtle baked in earth, and the flesh of a number of snakes.

Fittingly enough, our last stop was Acapulco, and there, like everybody else, we did nothing but lie in the sun and bathe in the sea and—for a little variety—go out deep-sea fishing once or twice. Acapulco nights are as busy and as amusing (and as effortless) as its days. I can not imagine a more suitable place in the world for anyone who would rather laze in the sun and store up his energy for future contingencies.

Mexico is much more than a place for lazing in the sun. That much I am sure of, despite the briefness of my stay in that strange and volatile country. As our plane took us back across the continent, I tried to sort out my final impressions—and found I was quite unable to make them neat and orderly. Mexico is simply too contradictory: not only the climate and the topography, the contrast between the very rich and the very poor, the strange mixture of lawlessness and religiosity (that is reminiscent of some of the rocky islands of the Mediterranean), the difference between the ancient timeless huts of the first sun-drenched settlers and the air-conditioned skyscrapers of the modern cities.

More than most countries, Mexico is a nation of unreconciled contrasts. Will they ever be reconciled? Odd facts and bits of knowledge kept flitting through my memory, as our plane winged onward toward the East: many of the people of Mexico are terribly poor, and their diet is dull and deficient—and yet they create some of the world's most highly prized handicraft and art. And their country, incidentally, is the world's largest producer of silver and one of the major suppliers of such semiprecious stones as opal, onyx, and jade. Being Japanese, I noted that although Mexico has thousands of miles of seacoast, it can boast neither a major fishing fleet nor one for merchant shipping.

Most important of all, perhaps: will the volatile and vital and creative nature of the people ever be reconciled with the fact that *mañana* is still one of their favorite words? I realized that in my short stay I had seen but a few of the many Mexicos that comprise this fabulous land, yet I do honestly believe that reconciliation is not only necessary but possible. I believe that the factors that breed poverty and illiteracy and violence can be eradicated—while at the

MEXICO

same time those other factors, the gentleness and kindness of the people, their endurance, their natural taste, their warmth, their dislike of endless bustle, need not be quite obliterated in the inevitable process. If that were to happen, not only Mexico but the whole world would be the poorer.

MEXICO

same time those other factors, the gentleness and kindness of the people, their endurance, their natural taste, their warmth, their dislike of endless bustle, need not be quite obliterated in the inevitable process. If that were to happen, not only Mexico but the whole world would be the poorer.

77. *Guadalajara*, the second largest city in the country, considers itself first when it comes to mariachis, Mexico's ubiquitous strolling musicians.

78–81. *The central market* of Guadalajara is the most fascinating in the country, with shops of all kinds and restaurants that are open from early morning till late at night, seven days a week.

82–85. *Religious pageantry* is part and parcel of daily life in Mexico and helps to enliven the hard, often drab existence of many of the poor. A religious festival calls for decking out the marketplace (upper left).

111

86–87. *Tlaquepaque*, an old, small village only two miles from Guadalajara, is famous for its cafés (lively at night, sleepy at noon) and its shops, which specialize in pottery.

88–90. *Tonalá*, just beyond Tlaque-paque, is a town of potters: their wares are not especially refined but are wonderfully refreshing after the dull precision of today's machine-made products. At left, a potter grinds glazing material.

91–92. *A religious sect* that flourishes in a Guadalajara suburb demands total abstinence of its adherents and also prohibits radio and television. Cameras are not allowed.

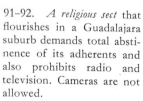

93–94. *Tequila* is not only the name of the national drink but also a town about forty miles northwest of Guadalajara; shown here, in Tequila, is the maguey plant from which tequila is distilled.

95–97. *El charro* is the name Mexicans give to these horsemen, who like to don their riding costumes on almost any pretext. Mexican women do not mind dressing up either.

98. *Typical village scene* at Capácuaro,
in Michoacán: while the girls work,
the men watch.

99. *Paracho*, also in Michoacán, specializes in the manufacture of guitars and other musical instruments; buyers come from all over Mexico.

100. *Wooden trays* are another specialty of Michoacán; inspiration comes from the flowers blooming in the district.

101. *Pátzcuaro* is the name of both
a Tarascan town (said to have been
founded in 1324) and the nearby lake,
where fishermen still use the old butterfly nets.

102–103. *Ancient Tarascan skills* survive in handicraft (right) and in the "Dance the Old Men" (below), performed on an island in the lake of Pátzcuaro.

104–105. *Taxco* is one of the prettiest
of Mexico's colonial towns and also
one of the most popular with tourists;
it lies squarely on the old road between the capital and the Pacific coast.

106. *Iguanas for sale!*
Armadillos are also
available from these
young shopkeepers
on the road to Aca-
pulco, not far from
Taxco.

107–10. *Not only in Taxco* but everywhere in Mexico, in every town and village, there are innumerable places for people to sit quietly, in sun or shade.

111–12. *Silver* is what originally gave Taxco its wealth, and although little is mined there now, the town has almost 200 shops selling silver to tourists.

113. *Pancho Villa*, a popular hero of the Revolution, stands in straw outside a folkcraft shop in Taxco.

114–16. *Acapulco* is many things to many people: an ancient seaport, a fishing village, a favorite with the jet set.

117. *Coconut palms* provide milk and meat, copra, oil, fiber—and shade for this elderly couple enjoying the sights of Acapulco.